Helen is a fun-loving woman who writes from the heart. Inspired by her son, she took up writing as a hobby. She now wants to share the poems she wrote with the public, demonstrating the feeling of deep and powerful emotion that went into her poems, some of which are based on her own experiences.

Helen Louise Porter

ENLIGHTENMENT

Poems

AUSTIN MACAULEY PUBLISHERS™

LONDON • CAMBRIDGE • NEW YORK • SHARJAH

A CIP catalogue record for this title is available from the British Library.

ISBN 9781788787635 (Paperback)
ISBN 9781788787642 (ePub e-book)

www.austinmacauley.com

First Published 2022
Austin Macauley Publishers Ltd
1 Canada Square
Canary Wharf
London
E14 5AA

I would like to thank my son.

POEMS

The Wings of a Dove

Fly to blue yonder
    Like a feather slowly
    Sinking to the ground.
    Flying gently, softly
Through the air.
Magnificent bird,
Like angels
Floating on a cloud
    Returning back to heaven
    Gently, softly.

Willow Tree

Willow tree,
How you make me feel
With the dropping of your
    Leaves,
Your hanging branches
    Loosely hung,
Your sweet smell of freedom,
    Lie loosely on the ground
    As they do,
As they do your branches
Swing back and forth
Like angels spreading
Their wings,
Only to be silent
Once again,
When the cool breeze
Disappears once more.

An Old Tramp...

An old tramp
Walked about the town
His boots all worn and torn.
His face looked so unhappy
And his coat was all patched up.
He laid down on a nearby bench
And covered himself
With paper.
The next day when I went there
The poor old thing had died.
He, slept in the wind, rain
And the snow
And now he's gone to heaven.
No longer shall he suffer
For now he's in God's arms
Where he will stay forever.

Hey, Mr Maker...

Hey, Mr Maker,
Can you make me a wooden cross,
So I may rest my head,
Lying deeply beneath the earth,
My spirit and soul returning
Back to God once more?
Thank you, Mr Maker.
Now I am at peace.

Shine Your Light

Shine your light upon
The earth,
Glistening stars

Brightly shone.

The heavens open.
The rain pours down,
Yet the stars still shine,
Floating next to the moon
In all its glory
And splendour.

The Day Passes Slowly

The day passes slowly.
The sweet smell of summer
Shines through the window,
Birds gently singing.
The sun shines bright.
Traffic goes past,
Eager to return to work,
Slowly returning
Back to normal.

You Said You Loved Me...

You said you loved me.
You said you cared.

You don't love nobody.
You had me fooled for
A while.
You've got my heart
Trapped in your soul.
You've got my heart
Trapped right in your
Soul.
You got that kid look
In your eyes.
You got your lipstick
All over your face.
You've got my heart
Trapped in your soul.
You've got my heart
Trapped right in your soul.

Angel Child

You're caring.
You're lovely.
Your smile,
Your golden hair,
Your chubby cheeks,
Beholden to you a
Glow of light
That sparkles
Like the stars.
Your inner soul
Shines light magic.
Your personality glows
Like saints
From heaven,
Who watch over us.
You are a special
Child.

Butterfly

With wings like angels
Spreading beautifully
    In the air,
Gliding swiftly
Backwards and forwards,
Flying in and out
    Of flower petals,
With the brisk warm air,
Retiring to a leafy hedge
Where settled,
Relaxed and peacefully rested,
A child lingers with a net,
Catches the beautiful
Butterfly only to let it
    Loose
Flying once again, in the
    Brisk warm air.

My Love for You...

My love for you
Will never end,
Like time itself
Never ending,
Going hopelessly on and on.
We will never be apart.
My love for you goes
   On and on.
     We will never be apart.
My love for you
Goes on and on,
Like a ticking clock
That never ends.
Farewell my love, farewell.

Summer Passes...

Summer passes
    Quickly now.
The dark shadows
That follow me
Bring new light
    And hope:
A new beginning,
A new world.

Glory Be...

Glory be,
Feeling much better!

Still bathing achy legs,
Least on water tabs.
The night draws on slowly.
Tomorrow looms,
Another day.

Tonight, Can't Sleep...

Tonight, can't sleep.
Sky's pitch black.
Not a star to be seen.
Is the earth crumbling
Beneath us?
Are dark shadows
Following us
In a strange way,
Only for the new
Morn
To come once more?

Looking Glass...

What do you see
When you look back
At me?
  Sad eyes,
  A lost smile,
  Gone so long ago,
  Hopefully to return
  Once more.
  Pain and suffering
  Looms around me,
  But new hope will reign
  Once more.

Hey, War Soldier...

Hey, war soldier,
Out in the desert
Fighting for Queen
And country,
Arms drawn in battle
Ready to steam
The enemy.
What enemy,
You may ask?
Covid 19, of course.

Hey, Mr Sunshine...

Hey, Mr Sunshine,
Bring me a smile
So wide
It swallows
Up hate, resentment
And shame,
Bringing peace
Once more to the earth.

Charity

Be loving,
Be giving,
Share with the poor,
Open your hearts.
If you see a man
In the street
With no coat
And no shoes,
Give generously
With open arms.
It could be you
With no coat, no shoes.

Oh My Secret Garden...

Oh my secret garden,
How I long to walk
The path of time,
Turn back the clock,
Unwind the time,
Return to a life
Where freedom
Was mine.
Looking through
The glass window,
Only to see beautiful trees,
A pathway
Out of my prison.

Rainbow

Rainbow, how I long
To see your glistening
Colour of pure splendour,
Spreading all your delights
Across the sky,
Opening the heavens
With all its glory,
Pouring beautiful rain,
Replenishing the earth,
    The trees,
    The plants,
    The grass,
    Making fresh,
    Making new.

It's a Misty Day

Your face was daunting,
The mist slowly
Gliding over the rocks.
    You stood there
    And love was mine.
I slowed down.
I saw your face.
The night dawns in.
You fled from me.
What happened
To love that was mine,
Lost so long ago?
Come back to me,
My darling do,
For you are forever
Mine.

A Pictured Sculpture

Your face was a pictured
Sculpture
In the moonlight.
You danced like
Shadows in the night.
You were perfect.
You were perfection.

My Heart Pierced...

My heart pierced,
It missed a beat.
You glanced at me
And went on by.
The distance had grown
But now we were
In perfect harmony.

Green Meadow

Green meadow
With grass, so green.
Buttercup, glistening
    In the wind.
A white rabbit
Appears from its hole,
Jumping free.
If only I could be so
    Free,
What a rich man
I would be.

Silence Is Golden

Not a pin drop
You can hear
But if only
I could hear
Your sweet voice
Your beautiful smile
How close we could be
But no silence
Was mine

They Say Lust...

They say lust
Is great,
But your passion
Is stronger than
Any kind of love,
Throws my heart into the extreme.
My heart beats
Beats like Big Ben,
The clock
Pounding for your love,
For only us to see.
Yes, I would say
Passion, is better
Than lust.

Angel Babies

Angel babies
Cuddling gently,
As wings
As white as snow,
Golden and brown hair,
With an expression
    Of pureness,

You are in heaven.
    God rest you
    And keep you.

Shirley

You and your family
Have been supreme.
You were there
    And you cared
No matter what.
You all mean
So much to me:
    Times of sadness,
    Times of joy,
    Times of trouble,
    Times of hate.
If I was alone,
    You wouldn't
    Have it.
You always made
    Me welcome.
You are truly
    One of a kind.

Glo

You are an angel
Among angels,
For the little angel
Upon your shoulder
Does protect you always.
For there are
    No wings
    Nor halo too,
    Just a shining light
That shines right through you,
Of goodness,
    Kindness too.
These are the things
    I see in you.
May all your hopes
And dreams come true.

Christmas Comes

Christmas comes
And brings
Much joy:
    Family
    Friends
    Fine wine
    Good spirits
    Churchgoers
    Singing to their
    Hearts' content;
The vicar
Praising the Lord
With such love
    And passion,
Bringing peace
And love
    Around the world.

CPSIA information can be obtained
at www.ICGtesting.com
Printed in the USA
LVHW020531010322
712195LV00010B/609